ANXIOUS ANNABELLE AND THE MYSTERIOUS 88 KEYS

JAZZY JOY

SWEETSPIRE LITERATURE
MANAGEMENT

TABLE OF CONTENTS

CHAPTER ONE

There once was a little girl called Annabelle. She was an inquisitive little girl who wanted to learn and explore the world.

First of all, Anxious Annabelle thought she'd like to be an astronaut and sail through space in a lovely red rocket. She'd stare at the planets and seek out new stars just like they did in Star Trek.

Annabelle knew that she would need to go to University and learn a lot of things before she could be an astronaut, so she thought again about a different adventure.

Next she imagined being an explorer and finding new lands, full of amazing creatures that she could tame. Her problem was she didn't own a boat or a plane, so she couldn't get to those magical lands.

Perhaps Annabelle could change her plan and find something new she could explore at home.

Annabelle knew her family owned a piano keyboard. Her mother played lovely tunes on that keyboard and Annabelle loved to hear them every day. She thought about that amazing maze of black dots and dashes on the music page and wondered how her mother made them into the beautiful pieces that she heard every day.

Suddenly she knew that this could be her Big Adventure. There were 88 keys to explore and millions of notes in pages of books that she could trek through on her quest.

CHAPTER TWO

Her mother found a piano teacher to help her with her adventure and the journey began.

First of all, her piano teacher, Mrs Jazzy Joy showed her a website. On that website were the names of all her piano students. Because it was her first day, Anxious Annabelle's name was at the bottom. This troubled Annabelle a little, as it was a long way to the top, at least 40 steps.

Mrs Jazzy Joy showed her all the ways that she could earn points, just like in a computer game. Firstly, she could practice every day. That was easy. Annabelle liked to get ahead, so that made sense and the most points were awarded for practising every day.

Next, Mrs Jazzy Joy suggested that she play her tunes to her grandparents as much as possible each week. Now this was a BIG problem to Annabelle and she made a huge frown.

Annabelle's grandparents lived all over the world. They didn't just live down the street like many Australian grandparents. Annabelle told her Mum and Dad about this dilemma and they smiled and said, "That's OK, Annabelle, we have the answer."

Instead of talking to your grandparents, we can use Messenger and they can see you play all your pieces. Of course, Annabelle's grandparents were overjoyed to hear about the idea. They missed seeing Annabelle and her brother and this way they could see them and hear their music too!! So, the magical, mysterious, musical journey would begin.

CHAPTER THREE

Anxious Annabelle went to her first piano lesson and learnt about Middle C. Mrs Jazzy Joy taught Annabelle that Middle C was in the middle of the piano keyboard. Of course, that made sense. So Middle C could be played by her Right Hand and it could be played by her Left Hand.

Annabelle thought about all the C's. It was just like imagining you were on the High Seas in a ship. The Big Adventure had started.

Annabelle imagined she was sailing on her Catamaran across the C sea to an island full of C's. She took her cat, named CC, she ate custard and cream and caught catfish to celebrate.

Mrs Jazzy Joy taught Annabelle about all the C's on the keyboard. There were 8 C's. Annabelle explored them all. Low C made a deep sound, just like caged carnivores. Bass C was a little better, just like a calling Cow. Then of course, there was Middle C, in the Middle. Next came Treble C, plenty of cackling corellas here. Up you went to High C, sounding like a cacophony of cute cicadas.

Annabelle had learnt so much just by exploring her C's. There she was in the middle of a great adventure and learning about everything she had imagined and even more. She was so excited to play to her grandparents and earn points so she could climb up that leaderboard past all those 40 students to the top. The climb was just beginning.

CHAPTER FOUR

When Anxious Annabelle went to her next piano lesson, Mrs Jazzy Joy told her about Middle G. This puzzled Annabelle because it would be usual to talk about D after C, like in the alphabet. "Not so," said Mrs Jazzy Joy, "G is next most important to C". It could be played by the Right Hand along with Middle C or with Left Hand playing Middle C. Now Annabelle could play both hands together. That's really exciting!!

That night Annabelle dreamt about the Land of G's. Golliwogs and girls, giraffes and geraniums. Galloping gazelles on glitzy glaciers pounded in her brain. Learning about G had really moved her imagination machine into high gear.

Every day Annabelle played her new pieces gaining confidence in playing and reading her notes. Every night her brain buzzed, full of new dreams about mystical creatures and magical boats. Next time Annabelle went to lesson, Mrs Jazzy Joy showed her that Left Hand would play Letter F. Annabelle could play Left Hand F then Right Hand C then Right Hand G or she could play all three at once! Oh! What a cacophony? Or is it a calamity? Anyway, it was quite noisy.

Days were filled with songs of 3 notes played in all combinations. Annabelle's nights were alive with dreams of fiddles and fishes, footballs and fairies. If ever Annabelle thought she needed an adventure, now she was so busy and excited and all inside her home without a boat or a plane.

CHAPTER FIVE

Annabelle went to her next lesson all happy and chirpy. She had practiced and played to her grandparents overseas. Annabelle was ready to perform to Mrs Jazzy Joy. All her pieces were played without a note wrong and her teacher recorded her points. Mrs Jazzy Joy explained that when Annabelle reached 1000, she would earn a gold coin. The website would show her special rewards to redeem with her coins. Annabelle went home with a new desire to earn points. There was such an amazing array of sparkling, shiny and special things. It looked very enticing to Annabelle's brain. It buzzed yet again.

Next to arrive were the D,E,F's in between C and G. Now that sent Annabelle into delighted dreams. Dogs on doors, elephants eating and frogs floating in great seas of glittery glass. This was most amazing for Annabelle the Explorer "I'm just like Dora", she thought. Mrs Jazzy Joy showed her how to play G, A and B. Finally!!

A and B before her C's, Annabelle was most pleased. Annabelle showed her parents, her brother and her grandparents all the glorious, gorgeous gymnastics she could perform. Annabelle played with one hand, one finger, two hands, three fingers. The combinations were confusing but very creative. Music came out creepy and catchy, dramatic and dreamy, fishy and FROZEN!!!!!!

Oh what a marvellous thing to be able to play FROZEN!!! All the world's magic rolled in one throw, when a little girl can play LET IT GO!!!!

Now her dreams were like being at the movies at night. Lovely lyrics, magical music dripping in icy icecream.

Heather Lucas Piano Lessons
Student of the Year 2019
Annabelle Mossford MacGregor

CHAPTER SIX

Annabelle had played so much and so often that Mrs Jazzy Joy was having trouble with her Maths. So many calculations for a piano teacher was very exhausting!! 43 pages times 50 points each equals???? Oh!!! this is too tough!!! Thank goodness the website can calculate well enough. "My brain is bursting", she blurted. Annabelle clambered at such a fine pace, that she zoomed right into outer space, leaving everyone in a daze. Annabelle played waltzes and walks, jingles and jangles, ballets and boogies. Way past Alla Turcas, Allegros, Andantes, Plundering Pirates and Marching moon men.

Annabelle worked feverishly forever, collecting medals and prizes, coins and trophies. Then came the Grand Fine (Feenay) Concert. Anxious Annabelle was anxious but excited about the concert. She knew her name was at the top. What would this mean at the Grand Fine (Feenay) Concert?

Anxiously she waited through all manner of songs. Pink Panther, Turning tables and even Momentum. Addams Family Theme, Oh, how she could scream. She waited past medals and trophies until the big moment when she was promoted. Suddenly she was Annabelle the Almighty, with a trophy most glorious and a voucher to spend.

Long gone was Annabelle the Anxious.

ABOUT THE AUTHOR

I have been teaching piano since I was sixteen.

I have met and taught many interesting students and have been inspired to write about some of the most outstanding students.

I have lived in rural Australia all of my life and love the peace and beauty of the landscape.

I have combined my love of painting, music teaching and the natural surroundings to create an inspiring story for children.

I have a husband, 2 children and 4 grandchildren.

www.ingramcontent.com/pod-product-compliance
Lightning Source LLC
Chambersburg PA
CBHW061148030426

42335CB00002B/147